Look at the people in the picture.
They are all wearing uniforms.
What are their jobs?

uniform

Now read about them.

This man is a pilot. He works at the airport and flies a big plane. His plane is very fast.

pilot

**cockpit**

**jacket**

Pilots sit in the cockpit of the plane.
It is very noisy in there.

Pilots wear jackets and hats.

THE BLUE CROSS

animal hospital

This man is a vet.
He works in an animal hospital.
He helps people's pets.
Vets give medicine to animals.

vet

Some vets help animals at the zoo.

They are not scared of dangerous animals.

Some vets wear white coats.

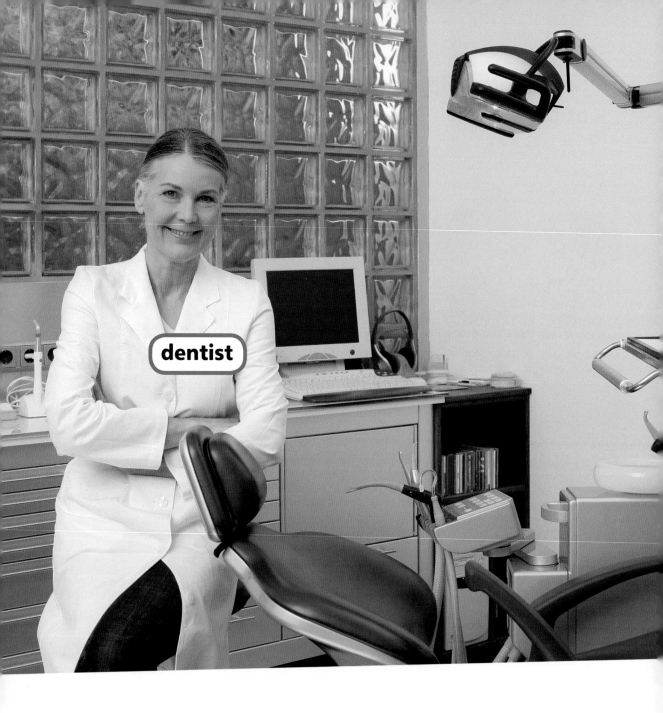

dentist

This woman is a dentist.
People visit her at a dentist's office.
She looks at people's teeth.

People sit in the dentist's big chair.
Dentists wear masks and gloves.

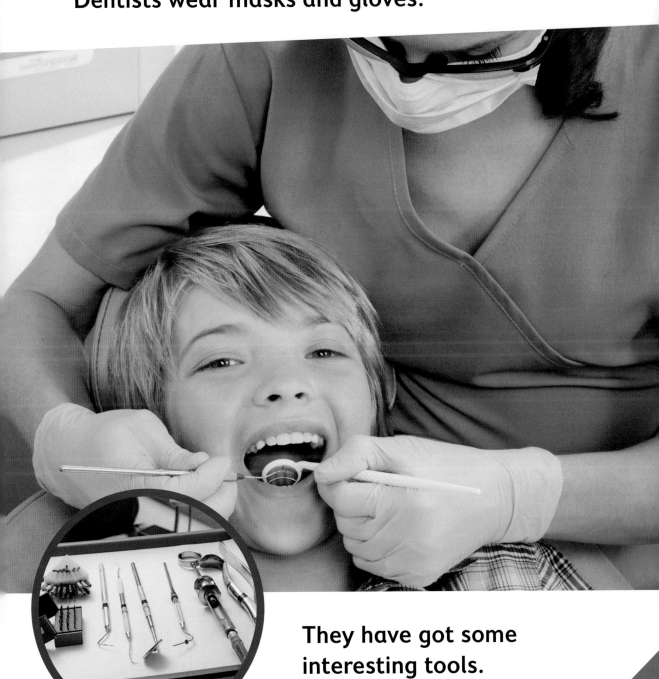

They have got some
interesting tools.

fire engine

firefighter

This man is a firefighter. He works at a fire station. He drives fire engines. It is a dangerous job.

Firefighters climb tall ladders and go in high buildings.

Firefighters wear big heavy coats, big hats and gloves.

ladder

This woman is a chef.
She works in a restaurant.
She makes breakfast, lunch
and dinner for hungry people.

chef

Some chefs are famous.
They make great food.
Chefs wear white shirts.
Some chefs wear tall white hats.

This man is a mechanic. He works at a garage. He knows a lot about cars.

mechanic

garage

SERVICE RECEPTION

BR

Mechanics work with interesting tools. They fix problems with cars and lorries.

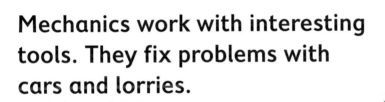

overalls

Mechanics wear overalls. Their overalls get very dirty!

This girl is a student. She goes to school every day.

She wears a uniform. What do you wear?

# Activities

## Before You Read

**1** **Read and match.**

chef    dentist    mechanic    pilot    vet    firefighter

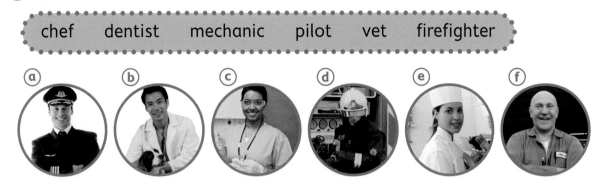

## After You Read

**1** **Read and match. Whose are they? Tell your friend.**

overalls    gloves    white coat    jacket    tall hat

**2** **Read, then write the job.**

1 A _____ flies a big plane.

2 A _____ fixes cars.

3 A _____ helps people's pets.

4 A _____ climbs tall ladders.

5 A _____ looks at people's teeth.

6 A _____ makes food in a kitchen.

**Pearson Education Limited**
Edinburgh Gate, Harlow,
Essex CM20 2JE, England
and Associated Companies throughout the world.

ISBN: 978-1-4082-8813-9

This edition first published by Pearson Education Ltd 2013
9 10
Text copyright © Pearson Education Ltd 2013

The moral rights of the author have been asserted
in accordance with the Copyright Designs and Patents Act 1988

Set in 19/23pt OT Fiendstar
Printed in China
SWTC/09

### Acknowledgements

The publisher would like to thank the following for their kind permission to reproduce their photographs:
(Key: b-bottom; c-centre; l-left; r-right; t-top)

**Alamy Images**: Andrew Aitchison 15t (d), Corbis Flirt 15t (f), Corbis Premium RF 1 (dentist), 1 (vet), 5b, 15 (b) geldi 9r, Geoff Wilkinson 4tl, MBI 12, 14, Mike Booth 5c, numb 11tr, Ron Niebrugge 5tr, SHOUT 9l, UpperCut Images 7c, Westend61 GmbH 3; **Corbis**: Con Tanasiuk / DesignPics 11b, DreamPictures / Pam Ostrow / Blend Images 4b, Drew Myers top (c), Paul Burns 7bl, Wolfgang Flamisch 6; **Fotolia.com**: auremar 13b, crolique 10br, Jacek Chabraszewski 10tr; **Getty Images**: Eric Nathan 8, James Lauritz 2r; **Shutterstock.com**: antos777 13t, auremar 1 (mechanic), bonchan 11tl, Deklofenak 15t (a), Kurhan 1 (chef), Pincasso 2l, RTimages 1 (pilot), T-Design 1 (firefighter); **SuperStock**: Pixtal 10l, 15t (e)
Cover images: *Front*: **Alamy Images**: Beautyfashion; *Back*: **Shutterstock.com**: auremar

All other images © Pearson Education

In some instances we have been unable to trace the owners of copyright material,
and we would appreciate any information that would enable us to do so.

Illustrations: Mark Ruffle

For a complete list of the titles available in the Pearson English Kids Readers series, please go to
www.pearsonenglishkidsreaders.com. Alternatively, write to your local Pearson Education office or to
Pearson English Readers Marketing Department, Pearson Education, Edinburgh Gate, Harlow, Essex CM202JE, England.